E

— is for —

Economics

E

— is for —

Economics

by

Veronica Goodman

Illustrations by
Nicole Jones Sturk

To S, with love

Text and illustrations copyright © 2018 by Veronica Goodman.

First Printing, 2018
ISBN 978-1-7320857-0-1

The images were created using vector design and the text was set in PT Serif Caption.

For more information about this book, please visit www.veronicagoodman.com.

A

is for Adam Smith

is for Boom and Bust

C is for Capital

is for
Demand

$e^{2x}(x^2+4x)e^x dx$

$Y=AL^{\alpha}K^{\beta}$

$x,y,\lambda)=f(x,y)-\lambda \cdot g(x,y)$

E

— is for —

Economics

$MR=mc$

$\alpha + x\beta = y$

$x\alpha + x^2\beta = xy$

Price

Equilibrium
$Q_d = Q_s$

supply

demand

Quantity

B

C

A

is for Fixed Costs

is for Households

J is for Jobs

K

is for
John
Maynard
Keynes

L is for Labor

M

is for

Monopoly

N

is for

Nash Equilibrium

O is for
Opportunity Cost

is for Price

Q is for Quantity

2.00 lbs

1.00 lbs

T is for Technology

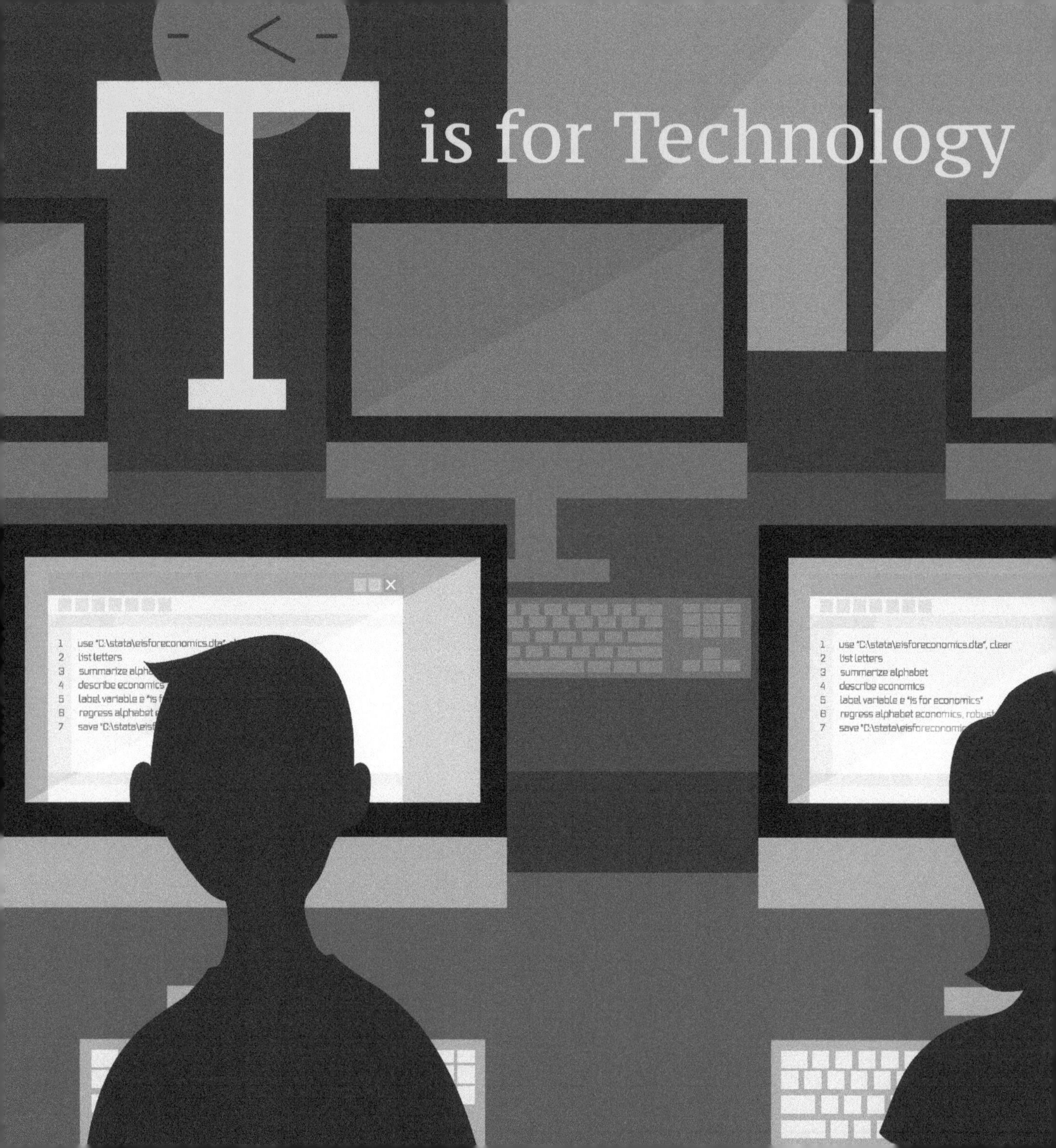

is for Utility

V is for Variable Costs

W is for Wages

is for
eXternalities

Y

is for
Janet
Yellen

Z

is
for
Zero
Sum